Is This My Church?

Faith and Feeling During a Church Merger

Ann Hopwood

Jungian Psychoanalyst

GROVE BOOKS LIMITED

RIDLEY HALL RD CAMBRIDGE CB3 9HU

Contents

Acknowledgments

I would like to thank the staff of Sarum College for their support and encouragement. Also the staff and members of the church I have called Newhaven for their willingness to share their experiences, especially SW and HB without whom the research would not have been possible. And my husband David for his love and unfailing support.

First Impression March 2020
ISSN 0144-171X
ISBN 978 1 78827 115 8

1

'It's as Though Part of My Heart's Gone'

How does the merging of two or more churches affect the individuals and groups involved? While church mergers are fairly common in today's world, much of what is written is intended to help church leaders in the mechanics of merger, and to avoid failure, but there is very little evidence of how these processes affect the people involved. A study of a local situation of the merger of five Methodist churches in Britain considered the feelings of the individuals and groups belonging to these churches and how they were affected during the project up to the time when it was completed. The study was carried out in a town called 'Bridgetown.'[1] The study suggests that paying careful attention to the psychological needs of individuals, as well as thinking about their spirituality and so the meaning and purpose for them of the project, affects the outcome. Group processes are also considered to be very important to the outcome, which in this instance led to considerable success.

Paying careful attention to the psychological needs of individuals affects the outcome

Following my retirement as a Jungian psychoanalyst, I began a Master's degree course in Christian Spirituality at Sarum College, Salisbury. Shortly before the time when I was considering my dissertation project, I had been involved, as a leader in the larger church, in a possible merger of the two Methodist churches in the town near where I live. One of the churches was rather small with a mainly elderly congregation, and the other, situated in the centre of the town, was bigger and livelier. The plan was for the members of the smaller church to join with the larger church in the town centre premises. For some years the discussions seemed to be proceeding reasonably well, when the smaller church suddenly decided against the merger. This decision set me thinking about what was happening in the minds and hearts of the people who had made an emphatic decision not to join with the larger church after several years of what seemed to be positive discussions. I began to think about the individual and group psychology of the people who made the decision, and how and to what extent their spirituality and sense of mission to the town played a part in their decision.

During my course at Sarum College, I had met the Methodist deacon who was working at the new Bridgetown church, so, spurred on by my thinking about the other, failed project, and through my contact, I received permission from the church council of the Bridgetown church to study the processes which had led up to the success of their merger. To that end I interviewed a number of people, most of whom had lived through the years of the merger.

Understanding Church Mergers

While this project is firmly based within the Methodist Church, the issues of declining, elderly congregations are common for most, if not all, denominations, and people's feelings about loss and displacement are commonly held and are likely to become issues in any church closure or merger. This booklet therefore aims to enable church leaders and members, regardless of denomination, to understand more about which issues are important in thinking about church mergers, and how success may be achieved.

The following quotation illustrates some of the feelings of grief experienced by a member of one church which had closed.

> It was built soon after the war and the concrete was not of good quality so we were continually having to point the walls, and then we found asbestos…but it was a kind of sacrament really, because the place has so many memories and they were soaked into the walls, if you know what I mean…We're leaving a building where our children were christened; friends' funerals were there. So all this kind of soaks into the fabric, so it's not just a matter of locking a door and walking off. There were tears at the last service…but it was a lovely service.

The loss of the church building is an important aspect of the grief felt by people when a church building is being closed. As the quotation illustrates, there are powerful memories that deepen and strengthen the psychological and spiritual ties to a place of worship which may have links stretching over several generations of worshippers.

It is not only the building itself which is imbued with power but the artefacts too, described by Sheldrake as 'symbols of the sacred.'[2] A member of a different church expressed it thus:

> I was depressed when I went there (after the church had been sold). The walls had been painted white, the pews had been taken out, the pulpit was gone, the organ was gone, even the cross was gone. It no longer held for me anything.

This second church building had been bought by a different denomination and was still used as a church, albeit with a different ethos. Clark suggests that the church building becomes 'a repository of personal memory held in material objects.'[3] These material objects include such things as communion vessels and Bibles. The need for stability and a sense of home in a church building and the need for familiar surroundings and valued artefacts, commonly felt by the people who were interviewed as part of the study, is very powerful and likely to be strengthened with the sense of risk and anxiety associated with the need to close churches and to move to an uncertain future.[4] For some, the move to a new church in a different part of the town proved too difficult. Some elderly people were unable to contemplate moving to a church away from their neighbourhood either because of physical frailty or because of having close links with a particular community. One person, who had moved to worship with a different denomination, said, 'I have always been one to worship in my own community.' Her links with her local community proved stronger than those to the church of which she had been a member for many years.

The Place of Grief

Grief in its variety of aspects is an expected reaction to loss, and Elisabeth Kübler-Ross's work on bereavement in her influential study *On Death and Dying* can be widened to include other forms of loss.[5] Kübler-Ross outlines five stages of grief that need to be negotiated successfully to enable new internal development to take place and for people to be able to move forward into a different future. These stages are: denial, anger, bargaining, depression and acceptance. Even earlier than the response of denial to loss is, for some people, a reaction of shock. 'It was a bombshell,' said one member. Some comments from people when they heard the news of the need to close their church were 'Over my dead body' and 'As long as the church is there for my funeral,' illustrating their reaction of denial in the face of loss. This reaction is likely to be closely followed by anger. One comment was that the superintendent minister overseeing the merger of the churches 'received all the brickbats,' illustrating a common reaction of blaming the messenger for bringing unwelcome news. Anger as a reaction to grief has the advantage for the individual that it may lend a feeling of power in the face of debilitating helplessness. Along with other aspects of grief, anger needs to be worked through in order for a good mourning process to be completed and a good resolution found.

Grief is an expected reaction to loss

In this study, the members of all five churches moved together to one church, known as Anderson Street, as an interim measure, while the church chosen to be the eventual home of the united congregation, Hexham Road, underwent complete refurbishment. When the time came to move into the new premises at Hexham Road, a number of the original members of Anderson Street saw no reason why they should not retain the Anderson Street building as a worship centre. There was a need to step out in faith but for some that was a very hard or even impossible thing to do. Kübler-Ross describes bargaining as a way of trying to delay or avoid the inevitable outcome thus:

> If we have been unable to face the sad facts...and have been angry at people and God...maybe we can succeed in entering into some sort of agreement which may postpone the inevitable happening.[6]

Bargaining by some of the original members of the Anderson Street church was perhaps strengthened because they had seen their church become 'more vibrant' again with the advent of the incomers. Some felt that worship should continue there and that the Hexham Street site be used purely as a community centre.

Depression is a very common and well understood reaction to grief but does carry within it the hope and likelihood of a resolution of the grief, since it implies an understanding of the reality of loss and a growing capacity to manage and survive it.[7] This leads to Kübler-Ross's final stage of acceptance.[8] In the case of the churches at Bridgetown, acceptance was accompanied by a more active understanding of a vision of a rebirth and a renewal of Methodist life in the town when several of the original churches involved in the merger were dying. By the time that the study was conducted, the acute phases of grief had been long worked through, or at least some accommodation had been reached with the situation. Hamman differentiates between grief and mourning, describing mourning as 'the intentional letting go of relationships, dreams, and visions...after the experience of loss and change.'[9] In other words, mourning denotes a successful working through of the process of grief.

Grief at the loss of churches was accompanied by the loss of friends

Grief at the loss of churches was also accompanied by the loss of friends who were unable to make the transition to the new building and so became more distant. Much work was done in the Bridgetown situation in visiting people to help them understand the developments and to offer them help in making the transition to the new building, but one member said, 'We left a number of people. We did our very best to bring them with us, by offering lifts, by talking, but not many made it.' Even after a considerable passage of time, the sense of upset was quite easily evoked during interviews when people remembered the loss of friends and difficult situations when people were left behind. For some, there was also a feeling of guilt as to whether enough had been done to maintain pastoral care for those who were left behind or who had joined churches of a different denomination.

Risk was one element of the difficulty people had in embracing the project. Someone said, 'There was no guarantee that we would not fall off the edge of a cliff,' and another, 'Some thought that it was too risky a risk.' The sense of risk of losing what had been precious to them without knowing whether they would be able to achieve their goal was at times disabling. Their goal was the major refurbishment of the church building at Hexham Road, which was virtually falling down and in need of a great deal of fundraising in order to ensure that it would fulfil the vision that was taking shape.

The reasons for the closing of churches are well known, with declining numbers, elderly congregations, difficulties in finding leadership, the need to maintain aging buildings and financial issues. The realisation of the need to close a church mitigated to some degree the sense of loss associated with it. One person thought that it was easier for members of the churches that were dying to contemplate their closure than for the two churches in the town which continued to have viable congregations.

Methodism was born in song and from earliest times Methodists have learned and expressed their theology and faith through the singing of hymns.[10] The churches in the study set considerable store by the part music plays in worship, and when it no longer became possible to maintain a reasonable standard of music, some people realized that the time had come to close the church, and included this aspect in their rationale for the closing of their church.

2 'We're On a Journey and We Don't Know Where it's Leading'

Congregations mourning the loss of their musical tradition are already in a situation of grief, and this is not a position from which change can easily come about. Change can often be seen as a threat rather than an opportunity when people are in a position of depression and weakness. In itself, change 'is often associated with anxiety, tension, and resistance.'[11] Marris argues that resistance to change is 'a fact of life,' and describes a 'conservative impulse' that is:

> ...as necessary to survival as adaptability: and indeed adaptability itself depends on it. For the ability to learn from experience relies on the stability of the interpretations by which we predict the pattern of events. We assimilate new experiences by placing them in the context of a familiar, reliable construction of reality.[12]

It follows that in order to be accommodated psychologically, change must take place within a context which is to some extent predictable and to which meaning can be attached. Resistance to change can be mastered when the individual has a secure enough internal foundation to welcome new challenges and experiences, and when there is sufficient continuity with what has gone before to enable them to accommodate the new within an existing framework of meaning.[13] This is a cumulative process, and the extent to which growth and change can be accommodated depends on the security of early attachments. Considered from this perspective, it would seem likely that people who are adequately mature psychologically should be able to accommodate a move to a different church building within the same denominational framework. However, as the comment 'We're on a journey and we don't know where it's leading' illustrates, the uncertainty and anxiety as to what the future will hold are likely to strengthen resistance to change.

Valuing What is Lost

Resistance to change does seem to increase with age, and so older congregations are more likely to find coping with major change difficult to envisage and to manage. In this context it is important that what is being lost in a merger continues to be valued. One person said that closing their church meant letting go of 'a very precious experience,' and another that people had 'very precious memories' of their previous churches and the memories the churches held for those who had belonged to them. One very elderly person had links to her church building extending as far back as her great grandfather in the nineteenth century. Writing as a psychiatrist, Cox suggests that Christian theology and practice are—in some areas of life—out of step with clinical experience, and that most Christian practice does not allow for what he describes as 'the lostness of loss.'[14] He suggests that the funeral service moves from death to resurrection without giving adequate time for grieving.[15] This may well be pertinent to the loss of a community and a church building, which may be followed rapidly by a celebratory church service once a move is completed, thus minimizing the sense of loss and grief for all concerned. Indeed it has been suggested by De Roest that leaders are inclined to move on too quickly because of being afraid of the extent and depth of feeling expressed by members of the congregation.[16] Alongside the need for time to express feelings, the congregations in the study did not lose sight of the need to pass on the baton of faith to subsequent generations. To achieve this, they knew that it was necessary to adapt to very significant change. Successful mergers, say Tomberlin and Bird, 'are vehicles of change, not preservers of the *status quo*.'[17]

Leaders are inclined to move on too quickly

Churches with dwindling and aging congregations are characterized by Tomberlin and Bird in *Better Together* as being in intensive care and they state that the merger of these churches typically fails 'because they are like drowning men clinging to each other.'[18] One local minister said that 'Strong churches don't think about merger,' and at least some of the churches in Bridgetown could be said to have been close to death.[19] Tomberlin and Bird suggest that churches which have faced many years of decline are 'often unable or unwilling to change.' They quote Mann as writing that congregations of this type spend too much time looking inwards and not enough on mission. They also say that the majority of mergers that fail come into the category that they describe as being 'in intensive care.'[20] They do suggest however that there are 'rare cases' where failing churches do begin to gain ground again following a merger.[21]

The merger at Bridgetown was initiated by the leadership, who decided to 'try and convince the five churches to catch a vision and come to a decision themselves to join.'[22] They were aware of a situation in a nearby town which had had a very unhappy outcome and were anxious to avoid such a thing happening in Bridgetown. An enterprise such as this cannot be undertaken as an exercise of power, and it is clearly critical to involve and encourage people in the undertaking. One person described the initial approach to the merger from the leadership as 'top down,' stating that it 'didn't work because it tended to put people's backs up.' Another person, however, said that they were led 'with great care, imagination and inspiration.' A meeting of members of all the churches was called, and from this meeting a consensus was reached for the members to work together on the project of creating one church and indeed 'catching the vision.' Many meetings were held in which fears and concerns could be shared, and prayer offered. Fears centred around differences in worship between the various churches, how pastoral care would continue to be managed, how easy transport would be to the new venue and where people would be able to park. The sharing of anxieties is obviously critical to a good outcome, as is a great deal of communication, making sure that people know and understand what is happening. Meetings were held with everyone sitting in a circle and with all being given the chance to speak and to express their fears and anxieties with much prayer.

The sharing of anxieties is critical to a good outcome

Valuing Individuals' Feelings

Little has been written in this country about church mergers, and research in the United States is not always directly relevant to situations in this country.[23] Tomberlin and Bird's study, however, gives some pointers which are relevant to churches in this country, and asserts that, in order to be successful, mergers need to be mission driven.[24] They suggest that 'The range of mergers include strong, stable, stuck, and struggling churches' and they give examples of a variety of different situations.[25] They describe change as an event, and continue that 'Transition is the emotional and psychological processing of the change.'[26] What they do not emphasize in any detail, however, is the importance of valuing the feelings of the people involved, and this holds true for other work on church merger in the United States.[27] Their emphasis is to help leaders in their task of merging churches. Although some mention is made of the need to grieve, there is little detail as to how people are likely to be affected and how these issues can be taken into account and given validity. This aspect was addressed much more directly in Buono and Bowditch's study of secular mergers, *The Human Side of Mergers and Acquisitions.* They cite Kübler-Ross's stages of grief and add that idealization of what is lost may also be present, meaning that the grieving person fails to make a significant enough attachment to what Buono and Bowditch call the new 'entity,' which in their case is an amalgamated firm.[28]

Cultural Differences

Buono and Bowditch also consider at length the issue of culture, particularly the need to understand the differing cultures represented in a merger and how they will affect the outcome. They outline two aspects of culture, the objective and the subjective:[29]

Subjective organizational culture refers to the pattern of beliefs, assumptions and expectations shared by organizational members and the group's characteristic way of perceiving the organization's environment and its values, norms, and roles as they exist outside the individual...[30] While '*objective organizational culture* refers to the artefacts created by an organization.'[31]

It is important in any situation of merger that the beliefs, assumptions and expectations intrinsic in the subjective culture are recognized as far as possible in each of the churches that plans to merge, so that they can be considered openly and, where possible, reconciled. While the formal organization and regulations of the Methodist Church are governed by *The Constitutional Practice and Discipline of the Methodist Church,* within these parameters local culture will inevitably have grown up in local congregations, and styles of worship and music may vary in different places and be strongly adhered to by members.[32] The two larger of the churches in Bridgetown were Ashley Road and Overton Street, and it was the differing culture of these two churches that was the most remarked upon in the study. Ashley Road was a rather traditional Methodist church while the members of Overton Street were more forward-looking and innovative. This clash of cultures created some issues which needed to be resolved. It was not all negative, however; one member of the Ashley Road church mentioned that worship had become 'vibrant' again following the coming together of the five churches.

Valuing Sacred Symbols

For churches, the artefacts inherent in their objective culture are likely to include Bibles, hymn books, crosses, communion vessels and war memorials and, importantly, their symbolic meaning for individuals and groups. Material goods carry meaning beyond themselves because they carry symbolic value. In the words of the psychiatrist Jung, the symbol 'express[es] the inexpressible in unsurpassable form.'[33] These articles therefore carry great meaning and value for individuals and groups and so need to be treated with considerable care and their significance recognized. In the case of the Bridgetown churches, artefacts which would be able to be used and displayed in the new church building were carefully stored, and those that could not be used were photographed so that their images remained for those for whom they continued to carry value.

Church buildings therefore carry not only psychological significance, but their significance extends to their spiritual value—church buildings and their contents are 'symbols of the sacred.'[34] Clark points out that from a theological point of view, church buildings are not significant, and that the word 'church' denotes its people, but there can be no doubt that from a psychological point of view, church buildings and their contents carry enormous significance in terms of the containment of memory and relationships. Clark highlights the 'religious memory' of buildings because of their connection with major life milestones—baptisms, marriages and funerals—and reminds us that many churches have 'multigenerational family ties.'[35] Clark cites Peter Read as stressing the importance of place in identity formation and development, and quotes him as writing that 'The meaningful events in our lives are inseparable from the places in which they occur.'[36] It is likely that the people who take part in the 'meaningful events' are also an inseparable part of the memories, and so are an integral aspect of what occurs within the walls of a church building.

Church buildings carry spiritual value

3 'You Can't See the Join'

It follows, then, that the working together of leaders and people was of the highest importance in the study of the Bridgetown merger, and the owning of the project and of their vision by the people was critical to its success. That is not to say that everything proceeded without difficulties. On one occasion, during a time of 'wavering and panic,' a member of the congregation, which was by that time united under one roof, is quoted as standing up in a meeting and saying, as a way of encouraging doubters, 'You all decided, you all agreed to this. Now that's it, we're here now; we've got to do it.' On another occasion, a minister encouraged all the congregation to stand if, however reluctantly, they were committed to the project. These illustrations point up the importance that the group process holds in any development of this kind.

Providing a Holding Environment

Many church communities provide a good holding environment within which it may be possible for change to take place. The concept of the holding environment was first formulated by Winnicott and refers to the way in which many small children use a comforter, known as a transitional object, as they begin to form an identity separate from that of the mother. The comforter helps to contain the anxieties of these very young, immature children as they begin to face the world. They usually grow out of this need as they mature. Winnicott, however, suggests that this 'intermediate area of experiencing'—that is, the transitional space—continues throughout life and in adult life is 'inherent in art and religion.'[37] Gaze suggests that church buildings act as transitional objects, and so act as a way of enabling people to contain their anxieties.[38] De Roest emphasizes that buildings carry more importance for people when they are about to be lost or when change is about to happen, and this concurs with Winnicott's theory as transitional phenomena are more likely to increase in prominence and carry more importance in the anxiety of impending loss.[39]

Hamman defines a holding environment as:

> The space created by a network of relationships within which people can tackle difficult and even divisive questions without flying apart… Within the holding environment one can address not only the difficul-

> ties that are experienced, but also the new difficulties as one addresses the hurdles that are impinging on a community.[40]

Shapiro and Carr go further:

> The holding environment, designed to provide empathic acknowledgement, containment, and perspective, forms a crucial dimension of all organizational and institutional life. Its loss in any context constitutes a serious deprivation and may contribute more to individual disturbance and to institutional irrationality and organizational disarray than has hitherto been recognized.[41]

During the development phase of the project at Bridgetown, many meetings were held with everyone being given the opportunity to speak. This did not mean that the project continued altogether smoothly and there is some evidence of the 'institutional irrationality and organizational disarray' alluded to by Shapiro and Carr.[42] After the move to the Anderson Street church, which was always intended to be temporary, members of one church brought with them a number of chairs. Discussions were held as to whether these chairs should be used to replace the pews at Anderson Street. The outcome of these discussions was that half the pews were taken out, with chairs being used in the space left vacant by the removal of the pews.

The containment aspect of holding is, in the context of the loss of a church building, clearly symbolized by the building itself, although the less tangible aspects of containment must also be of critical importance in the possibility of a change of venue taking place. An understanding of the need for change, of a different understanding of their mission—which many people in the study acknowledged—and the mutual support that they received from each other and from their leaders, would also have played a crucial part in their sense of continuing containment and support. Shapiro and Carr suggest that the need for holding may be addressed 'through ritualized symbolic structures that enable chaotic experiences to be faced.'[43] They go on to say that:

> Religious institutions, through their use of ritual and symbols, may facilitate a contained and managed regression for individuals and for larger groups to enable them to deal with problematic feelings and experiences in a constructive rather than a chaotic manner.[44]

Regression to a less developed internal state of being is likely to happen in situations of stress such as bereavement and uncertainty and, as Shapiro and Carr imply, this regression can be supported and managed more easily within groups which have a common purpose and a strong cohesion.

Culture and Community

Worship services and other forms of Christian devotion all played a part in enabling problematic feelings and experiences to be managed constructively for many people and to enable an imaginative project to take shape. Ostow suggests that the 'sense of fellowship that accompanies communal worship should not be considered a secondary aspect of the worship service,' and this sense of fellowship is an aspect of life together which Methodists prize highly.[45] The singing of hymns and songs, for instance, as well as reading long-cherished words together, cements this sense of fellowship and of belonging to one another.

This mutual support and belonging together is often carried out through a strong pastoral network which forms an important part of many Methodist churches. Shier-Jones goes so far as to describe it as an 'important dimension of Methodism's theology of membership,' and Methodists are called to 'support others in their discipleship.'[46] This was carried out faithfully by people being visited at home, and support and help was offered to further the possibility of people being able to overcome their misgivings and become part of the developing church community.

It was noticeable how empathic most of the interviewees were with their colleagues from different churches, which suggests—following Shapiro and Carr—'empathic interpretation' and 'valuing the experiences of others.'[47] It also implies a level of psychological maturity which is able to see beyond individual and immediate needs and to empathize in a loving way with other people, with their needs and their grief. One person noticed that the two churches which remained viable 'had to give up a lot more than Shelton Street because Shelton Street was dying. In a way, it was easier [for us].' The very successful outcome of the new development implies that a good enough holding environment was in place to enable the losses to be mourned, and to allow the anger and disappointment to be managed in such a way as to enable the possibility of development for individuals and groups.

Issues of culture also need to be worked through. The illustration above about the difficulty of deciding between pews and chairs indicates that the two congregations involved had not resolved their differing cultural issues. Local culture will inevitably have grown up in a cohesive and close-knit group of people, and styles of worship and ways of being together may differ in different places and will need to be thought about carefully and where possible reconciled. Tomberlin and Bird conclude that:

> Mergers have the best chance of success when there is at least an 80 per cent match in doctrine, philosophy of ministry, and ministry style.[48]

It is very likely that this match pertained in the study in spite of the issues of culture clash which became evident. The holding environment will have played a crucial part in the possibility of a new group of people coming together and working through the differences in their respective cultures. The result was, as one person who had joined the church after the merger said, 'You can't see the join and nobody goes on about it.' The new congregation has been able to see itself as one new congregation with a new culture and a renewed mission under God, even though the members continue to retain fond memories of their previous churches and of their importance in their spiritual lives and development.

'God is Doing Something New' 4

The people involved in the study were determined to develop the site of the one church that was situated in the centre of Bridgetown and which had large enough premises to accommodate the imaginative ideas that they envisaged. This major project was sustained by the hard work and faith of the people involved. When the study was being done, the new building was almost complete and had been renamed 'Newhaven.' The new name symbolized a new identity and the expectation of stepping out in faith into a new future. Tomberlin and Bird quote Tom Bandy as saying that in his experience 'Missional mergers depend on awakening the experience of Christ in the hearts of at least 20 per cent of the members of each church.'[49] It is not clear that this applied to each church in Bridgetown, but there were sufficient lay leaders who had caught the vision, were convinced that they were doing the will of God, and understood the need for mission. They believed that God was taking them into a new future. This enabled many others to follow and to share the excitement and gratification at the time when the new building was almost complete.

Worship and Mission

Worship was of course central to the enterprise and a new worship space was created on the first floor at the level of the former gallery of the nineteenth-century church building. This allowed flexibility and the possibility of experimenting with different forms of worship. There was some anxiety among older members at the loss of an organ to accompany worship, another loss that for some needed to be accommodated. For this group of Christians, worshipping and singing together had been important psychological and spiritual factors in their continuing growth as a community. Hymns and songs have always been a central way for Methodists to learn and express their faith. Maizel-Long writes that:

> Successive hymn-books were the way in which Methodists learned Christian doctrine, expressed the liturgical response of the congregation in public worship, grounded their daily devotions, and grew in faith and understanding.[50]

Music, especially music sung in groups with others, has the capacity to reach depths within the individual psyche and body. It plays an important function in deepening communal ties and bringing people as a group nearer to an appreciation of the divine, bringing together mind and psyche, soul and spirit.

Morisy suggests that the mission of the church 'is to be the body of people which, through the grace of God, participates in the initiatives which God takes in the world.'[51] In line with this statement, commitment to service to the community was the main motivation for making use of the site of the former Hexham Street church as a venue for the united church because of its location in the centre of the town. It is situated on a main shopping street, and is within sight of an area of deprived housing, thus catering for differing needs. Being in a location ideal for caring for those seen to be in need in the local community, was and is seen to be a crucial aspect of the mission of the church. It was an important feature of the planning, even though it might have been more advantageous financially to have settled on one of the other church buildings. It was envisioned from the outset that the new church building would be able to accommodate more than just the worshipping community, and the first enterprise which began in the building, long before it was completely finished, was a café. The café occupies a large space on the ground floor that had once been the sanctuary. It is a community café, staffed 'as a supported skills project for people with learning challenges' and offering a welcoming and friendly space to the community.[52] There is a play space so that mothers can meet each other secure in the knowledge that their children can play safely. Other rooms are let to a variety of community and statutory groups so that the building is open all week and in constant use. These outreach activities are seen as part of the mission of the church. One member described it thus:

> Christianity is about community and about people. That is what Methodists feel. It can't just be church, it has to be a community project and encompass all the people that are in the community and look at what their needs are at that time.

An article in a local magazine, written by a church member, also highlights the importance of outreach and community involvement as part of the spirituality of Methodist people:

> Methodism is founded on the social gospel. It asks what are we going to do about the people outside the building and the answer is to bring them in. [Newhaven] is one of [Bridgetown's] most socially deprived wards with large populations of families with young children and elderly people. It's part of our mission remit to counter social isolation, so the café with its play area is affordable and welcoming, a safe place, and Deacon [S] is often on hand to talk to people and where possible to signpost them to services.[53]

The deacon mentioned above, whom I had met before embarking on the project, was appointed to work with the community. She initiated a number of projects to this end which have reached groups of people previously unreached by the church.

Journeying From Home

It is clear that for church people, a sense of home—symbolized by a church building—is of considerable importance psychologically. Indeed, a senior member of the church mentioned at the beginning of chapter one, that had decided against the merger with a larger church, said that 'They [that is the church members] saw no reason to leave their home.' In this instance, the desire of the church members to remain together in a particular building overrode the risk of leaving home and venturing out as a way of furthering the mission of which they would have become part in a newly merged congregation. Home is a place from which to explore, a place that can enable a sense of security which may free one to take risks in the outside world, or else it is a place of retreat, and so a place of confinement and constriction that stifles growth. De Roest states that:

> The message of the 'placelessness' of the Christian faith, no matter how inspirational that may sound, is at odds with the psychological as well as spiritual need of congregations and the individuals within them to cling to their sense of place and the memories that place carries.[54]

The psychological and spiritual needs for a home can be mitigated when the individual has a secure enough sense of themselves and of an internal home to venture into new territory. Alongside the need for security, there is also a psychological need to explore and to develop, and a spiritual need to further the kingdom of God. In the case of Bridgetown, the Exodus story was used as an analogy for the journey the people were on, perhaps allowing them to be 'People of the Way' who would eventually have a home of their own and who could believe that their move was 'the future God is taking us into, stressful though it is.' Their journey was seen as 'God's requirement and challenge.' Like the Israelites, 'they journeyed by stages'—the people of Bridgetown remained in their temporary home in the Anderson Street church for as long as six years (Exod 17.1).

In the Exodus story, one can discern the psychological and spiritual unease of the Israelites in the wilderness. They yearn for what they remember as the fleshpots of Egypt, and rail against their hunger and thirst in the desert (Exod 16.3). In other words, they yearn for the only home they have known, and find the sense of rootlessness, which must have been very evident in the wilderness, extremely hard to bear. Later they make a golden calf to worship, feeling insecure without a God whom they could see and touch (Exod 32.4). Material attributes continue to have profound resonance in people's spirituality and so need to be attended to with care and respect.

Speaking of a sense of journeying that she sees as particularly characteristic of the Methodist people, Shier-Jones writes the following:

> In a very real way…it is appropriate to describe Methodists as a pilgrim people who never quite seem to believe that they are at their journey's end. This is evident in every aspect of their proclamation; the understanding of salvation as a process rather than an event, for example, or the constant search for church unity and reconciliation, and the conviction of the necessity and reality of God's calling to his people. It is implicit in the fact that the church defines itself in terms of a 'calling' rather than a 'being.'[55]

The tension between the psychological and spiritual needs to remain at home and the imperative to journey into God's future is very stark when there is a need to close churches and journey into something new and unknown. In the case of the churches in Bridgetown, the process slowly gathered momentum and was described by a member who had joined the church after the churches had come together in this way:

> They knew it wasn't sustainable, so they knew they had to do something about it, because the vision was that they were going to help more people this way, and reach out to more people as God wanted, not on their own in a little huddle.

It is probably only from the security of a tangible home that the concept of journeying can be accommodated, but the sense of home is not only encompassed by a physical building—it is also seen in the holding environment mentioned earlier. When a group of people feel themselves to be a strong community, they are more likely to be able to bear the uncertainty of moving to a new and little-known place.

Maintaining a Trajectory of Hope

Tomberlin and Bird assert that the majority of mergers that fail do so because they fall into what they call the ICU category.[56] Three of the Bridgetown churches probably fell into this category, including the Hexham Street church—where the membership was very low and the nineteenth-century building in an extremely poor state of repair. The remaining two, Overton Street and

Ashley Road, were still viable, although they too were experiencing some difficulties. In order for mergers in the ICU category to succeed and for the churches to gain ground, Tomberlin and Bird suggest that they need a 'new unified vision, new growth-minded leader, new location, and a new name.'[57] In the case of Newhaven, several of these issues were addressed, with the church being renamed following a ballot of members and a new vision found and carried through. The location of the united church is indeed the location of one of the former churches but it is so transformed, because the interior has been completely remodelled, as to have become a new and perhaps almost unrecognisable entity.

The innate conservatism and reluctance to change of at least some church members did not prevent the forward momentum because the majority were able to catch and maintain a trajectory of hope.

The study outlined here was a small one in a particular town, but it may contain pointers for people in other situations who find themselves in a situation not dissimilar from that which pertained in Bridgetown. Some of the research carried out in the United States suggests that mergers often meet with failure. That the outcome at Newhaven has been such a positive life-affirming one speaks highly for the people who have been involved in the project over a considerable number of years.

The initial discussions about the merger seem to have been based on the undoubted decline in the number of members and adherents of the Methodist church in the town and the realization that this was set to continue unless drastic action was taken, and that it would in time have led to the demise of Methodism in Bridgetown.

Everyone had to understand that God was leading them into something new

Each of the church councils and each member had the task of reaching a decision about closing churches and moving together. Everyone had to deal with the feelings associated with the decision as well as understanding the rationale and the way in which God was leading them into something new. The timing of their final move was not clear because of the decision to undertake extensive rebuilding and refurbishment work at the Hexham Street church. This meant that the united congregation began to meet in the Ashley Road church building temporarily, and it was a number of years before it became possible to move to their permanent site, which was renamed Newhaven.

Some of the issues that this group of people faced have been outlined. These include a good holding environment, the necessity for group cohesion and support, for commitment and persistence on the part of individuals, and for faith that they were doing what God wanted them to do, so that a good outcome could be achieved. At an individual level, each person must have worked through the stages of grief and mourning and become able to face the new challenges that were confronting them in an unknown environment, in order to reach the position in which they now find themselves. They now have a renewed, renovated church with additional facilities of a high standard, a much higher profile in the town, and the sense that they are now a people serving their community and using their 'resources to support the church in its mission in the world.'[58]

The issues that the Bridgetown Methodists faced were formidable and did not by any means guarantee a good outcome. They knew that they were taking a risk. Several of the studies of mergers in the United States suggest that declining congregations do not make for successful mergers.[59] The loss of members was expected; again, research in the United States anticipates a loss of 10–15% of the combined membership.[60] I have no figures to assess the extent of loss in the Bridgetown merger, although it seems unlikely to be as high as fifteen per cent. Anecdotally, the total membership of the five churches before the merger was about 150, and approximately the same number attended the first joint service on Easter Day. The gain of new members, which include families with children, has made up for the loss, at least in numerical terms.

Just as the Israelites encountered many difficulties in their wilderness years, so difficulties arose for the members of the Bridgetown church. These sprang from three separate issues. First, the decision to move all the members to the Hexham Road church, which a number of the people at Anderson Street thought unnecessary, and felt that the Anderson Street premises should remain open as a worship venue. A number of the members of the church council at Anderson Street are said to have resigned their posts, suggesting a level of disagreement with the plan that had previously been decided upon by representatives of all the churches involved. Secondly, new members coming from other churches began to suggest, or indeed to bring about, changes at Anderson Street which were not always welcomed by the original members there. A third issue was that a great deal of money needed to be raised to restore the Hexham Street church to a state in which it could become a facility fit for the purposes which were proposed. The money was raised partly from the sale of the closed churches and also from a great many fund-raising efforts and applications for grant aid. The hoped-for outcome was that the new church would become a beacon of hope for the community and a welcoming and open space for many groups, as well as a place of worship.

The hoped-for outcome was that the new church would become a beacon of hope

A considerable number of years have elapsed since the inception of the project, during which time a number of members have died or moved away, or indeed, in Methodist parlance 'ceased to meet.' A Service of Memory was held at the newly completed sanctuary to remember those people, and perhaps implicitly to enable the present congregation to move on with their current mission to be a centre of Methodist worship and outreach in the town centre.

Perhaps the most important requirement for a successful merger, and one which is evident in the Bridgetown situation, is that the majority of lay people are able to own the vision and commit to the changes that will occur and which they themselves will need to bring about, with all that that involves in terms of planning the project. This needs to be done within a context which has meaning and purpose for those involved. Careful attention needs to be paid to the concerns of individuals and groups as the process develops, so that as many as possible continue to be held within the worshipping community.

For those who have been able to stay the course and embrace the vision of the new worship centre and community facility, the move from Anderson Street to Hexham Road, now Newhaven, and the beginning of the town centre ministry, even in a building that was not yet complete, must have been a heartening experience. The individuals and groups involved have overcome a number of hurdles, both psychologically and spiritually, in order to reach the point that they have reached. They are now aware of the need to consolidate the work they have begun and to develop their mission and their spirituality in the place where they have chosen to be, and where they trust God to make use of them in this new way.

A member summed up the journey in this way:

> Was the slowness of steady meetings, prayer, understanding enthusiasm and dismay, pastoral care along the way, to bring people into one community—the right way to go forward? Yes! I feel confident that it would not have ended up with the positive atmosphere you feel in and around Bridgetown Methodists and Newhaven today if it had been led in any other way from the beginning.

Points for Reflection

In summary, the factors that make for success or failure in such a venture as that undertaken at Bridgetown include:

- The need to allow for and even to encourage grieving and mourning for what is being lost, in the sense of buildings and artefacts which are of such psychological and spiritual value to people and carry important symbolic meaning. There needs to be careful preservation of artefacts that can be incorporated into a new or existing building, and photographic evidence of what cannot be kept in material form. In addition, the crucially important intangible losses—such as those of friendships and links in a local community—need also to be mourned.

- The importance of a vision for the future under God being owned and understood by the vast majority of the people concerned, not just by the leaders.
- The importance of change taking place within a context that is meaningful to those involved.
- A strong communal sense and a sound holding environment, in which feelings both positive and negative can be expressed freely and worked through.
- A recognition and acceptance of cultural differences.
- The importance of a robust and flexible system of pastoral care, which includes those who may not be able to make the transition.
- A working through of the tension between the need for a home and the imperative to be a journeying people.

Notes

1 The names of the town and those of the churches have been changed for purposes of confidentiality.

2 P F Sheldrake, *Explorations in Spirituality* (New York: Paulist Press, 2010) p 178.

3 J Clark, '"This Special Shell"—The Church Building and the Embodiment of Memory,' *Journal of Religious History,* 31(1) 59–77, https://onlinelibrary.wiley.com/loi/14679809/year/2007 pp 66–67.

4 H De Roest, '"Losing a Common Space to Connect," An Inquiry into Inside Perspectives on Church Closure Using Visual Methods,' *International Journal of Practical Theology, 17(2)* pp 292–313, https://www.degruyter.com/view/j/ijpt-2013-17-issue-2/ijpt-2013-0018/ijpt-2013-0018.xml

5 E Kübler-Ross, *On Death and Dying* (London: Tavistock Publications, 1970) p 12. C Murray Parkes, *Bereavement: Studies of Grief in Adult Life* (Harmondsworth: Penguin Books, 1975) p 212.

6 Kübler-Ross, *op cit,* p 72.

7 D W Winnicott, *The Maturational Processes and the Facilitating Environment* (London: The Hogarth Press, 1985) p 241.

8 Kübler-Ross, *op cit,* p 12.

9 J J Hamman, *When Steeples Cry: Leading Congregations Through Loss and Change* (Cleveland: The Pilgrim Press, 2005) p 13.

10 *The Methodist Hymn Book* (London: Methodist Conference Office, 1933) Preface.

11 A F Buono and J L Bowditch, *The Human Side of Mergers and Acquisitions* (San Francisco, CA: Jossey-Bass Inc, 1989) p 108.

12 P Marris, *Loss and Change* (London: Routledge and Kegan Paul, 1986) p 6.

13 *ibid,* pp 19–21.

14 M Cox, 'A good-enough God? Some psychology-theology crossing places,' in S M Stein (ed), *Beyond Belief, Psychotherapy and Religion* (London: Karnac Books, 1999) p 57.

15 *ibid,* p 57.

16 De Roest, *op cit,* p 293.

17 J Tomberlin and W Bird, *Better Together* (San Francisco, CA: Jossey-Bass, 2012) p 91.

18 *ibid,* p 32.

19 Personal communication.

20 Tomberlin and Bird, *op cit,* p 33.

21 Tomberlin and Bird, *op cit,* p 32.

22 Personal communication.

23 The exception is Andy Griffiths' *Church Merger: When Two Became One* (Grove Pastoral booklet P132).

24 Tomberlin and Bird, *op cit.*

25 Tomberlin and Bird, *op cit,* p 5.

26 Tomberlin and Bird, *op cit,* p 100.

27 D Elliott, *Vital Merger* (United States: Fun and Done Press, 2013); R A Laribee Jr, 'Church Merger: Factors contributing to success or failure in congregational mergers' (2011), available at: https://www.amazon.co.uk/Church-Merger-Richard-Laribeeebook/dp/B004PVSOIA/ref=sr_1_1?keywords=Laribee&qid=156112; M Rogers, *Mergers* (USA: Equip to Grow Press, 2016); Tomberlin and Bird, *op cit.*

28 Buono and Bowditch, *op cit,* p 116.

29 Buono and Bowditch, *op cit,* pp 136–139.

30 Buono and Bowditch, *op cit,* p 139.

31 Buono and Bowditch, *op cit,* p 138.

32 *The Constitutional Practice and Discipline of the Methodist Church* (London: Methodist Publishing, 2018).

33 C G Jung, *Psychological Types CW6* (London: Routledge and Kegan Paul, 1971) p 475.

34 Sheldrake, *op cit,* p 178.

35 Clark, *op cit,* p 60.

36 Clark, *op cit,* p 73.

37 Winnicott, *Through Paediatrics to Psychoanalysis* (London: Karnac Books, 1992) p 26.

38 S Gaze, *Mission-shaped and Rural* (London: Church House Publishing, 2006) p 95.

39 De Roest, *op cit,* p 293.

40 Hamman, *op cit,* p 39.

41 E R Shapiro and A W Carr, *Lost in Familiar Places* (New Haven and London: Yale University Press, 1991) p 49.

42 Shapiro and Carr, *op cit,* p 49.

43 Shapiro and Carr, *op cit,* p 159.

44 Shapiro and Carr, *op cit,* p 159.

45 M Ostow, *Spirit, Mind, and Brain* (New York: Columbia University Press, 2006) p 62.

46 A Shier-Jones, *A Work in Progress: Methodists Doing Theology* (Peterborough: Epworth Press, 2005) p 243; Methodist Church, *Our Calling* (London: Methodist Church House, 2018).

47 Shapiro and Carr, *op cit,* p 7.

48 Tomberlin and Bird, *op cit,* p 98.

49 Tomberlin and Bird, *op cit,* p 180.

50 J Maizel-Long, 'Theology Sung and Celebrated,' in C Marsh, B Beck, A Shier-Jones and H Wareing (eds) *Unmasking Methodist Theology* (London: Continuum, 2004) p 48.

51 A Morisy, *Beyond the Good Samaritan* (London: Mowbray, 1997) p 2.

52 *The [County] Magazine,* 2018/2019.

53 *The [County] Magazine,* 2018/2019.

54 De Roest, *op cit,* p 331.

55 Shier-Jones, *op cit,* p 195.

56 Tomberlin and Bird, *op cit,* p 31.

57 Tomberlin and Bird, *op cit,* p 32.

58 Methodist Church, *Our Calling, op cit.*

59 Laribee, *op cit,* Introduction, and Tomberlin and Bird, *op cit,* p 21.

60 Elliott, *op cit,* p 82.